Chloe

AND THE CAT THAT NAPPED

A JOURNEY PUBLISHING BOOK
ISBN: 978-1-998473-05-2
Copyright © Shea Peterson 2025
Published by Journey Publishing
7-2070 Harvey Ave, Unit 156,
Kelowna,BC Canada V1Y 8P8
journeypublishing.net

Chloe
AND THE CAT THAT NAPPED

WRITTEN BY
SHEA PETERSON

ILLUSTRATED BY
MONIKA WNEK

Under cozy, warm blankets the sweet kitty purred.
She slept and she slept, and never stirred.
Not when the birdies chirped songs in the trees,
Not even when Chloe knelt down on her knees
and offered her treats straight from her hand.
Chloe pet little Snickers. "Kitty, I understand."

She didn't know why Snickers wanted to sleep.
Chloe would rather play than snore or count sheep.
"Mommy, Snickers just sleeps all day and all night.
I gave her treats and toys; something's not right."

"Snickers feels tired. She's trying to rest.
Just let her sleep. That's probably best."
Chloe reached out her hand to give kitty a pat,
But Snickers was startled. It upset the cat.

"We have to be kind and gentle to Snickers."
She stretched and she purred and wiggled her whiskers.
Chloe skipped off to play and hoped Snickers would, too.
With a world of adventure, there's plenty to do.

She launched a space mission of bears off to Mars,
who landed on planets among distant stars.

She trained a circus of elephants in big, round tents.
They trumpeted loudly for the ladies and gents.

She took to the runway as the next fashion queen.
Her style was the coolest Paris had seen.
Then, all of a sudden, the sun started to set.
"Snickers is home waiting for me, I bet!"
Chloe left her bears, circus, and fashion behind.
She ran to her room to see what she would find.

Would Snickers be sleeping or ready to play?
She needed to know now; she'd waited all day!
When Chloe pulled back the blankets, what did she see?
Snickers wasn't there! Oh, where could that kitty be?

She looked high and low. She looked up, down, and around.
She looked in every cabinet; Snickers couldn't be found.
"Snickers is missing, Mommy! I can't find my pet!"
"We'll find her, sweet Chloe. Now get ready for bed."

Later that night, by the light of the moon,
Chloe heard soft meows coming from her room.
It was muffled and quiet, she couldn't quite hear.
As she walked around looking; the sound became clear.

It wasn't just one meow. No, Chloe heard two!
Then another, and another! It was a whole zoo!
Chloe opened the closet and there on the floor,
lay Snickers with her kittens! One, two, three, and four!

Mommy came running. "Wow! What a surprise!
Snickers had kittens! I can't believe my eyes."
As softly and slowly as Chloe could muster,
She pet each one with care, so Snickers could trust her.

"Mommy, we have to be so kind and gentle, right?"
Chloe's smile glowed warmly; her eyes glistened bright.
"The kitties are tired. Let them sleep for a while."
She was proud of her daughter and gave her a smile.
"How did you get to be so smart, my girl?"
"I learned from you—the best Mommy in the world."
Snickers and her kittens slept soundly and happily,
knowing that they'd joined a kind and gentle family.

SNICKERS HAD ANOTHER LITTER! HELP CHLOE'S MOMMY COUNT THE KITTIES!

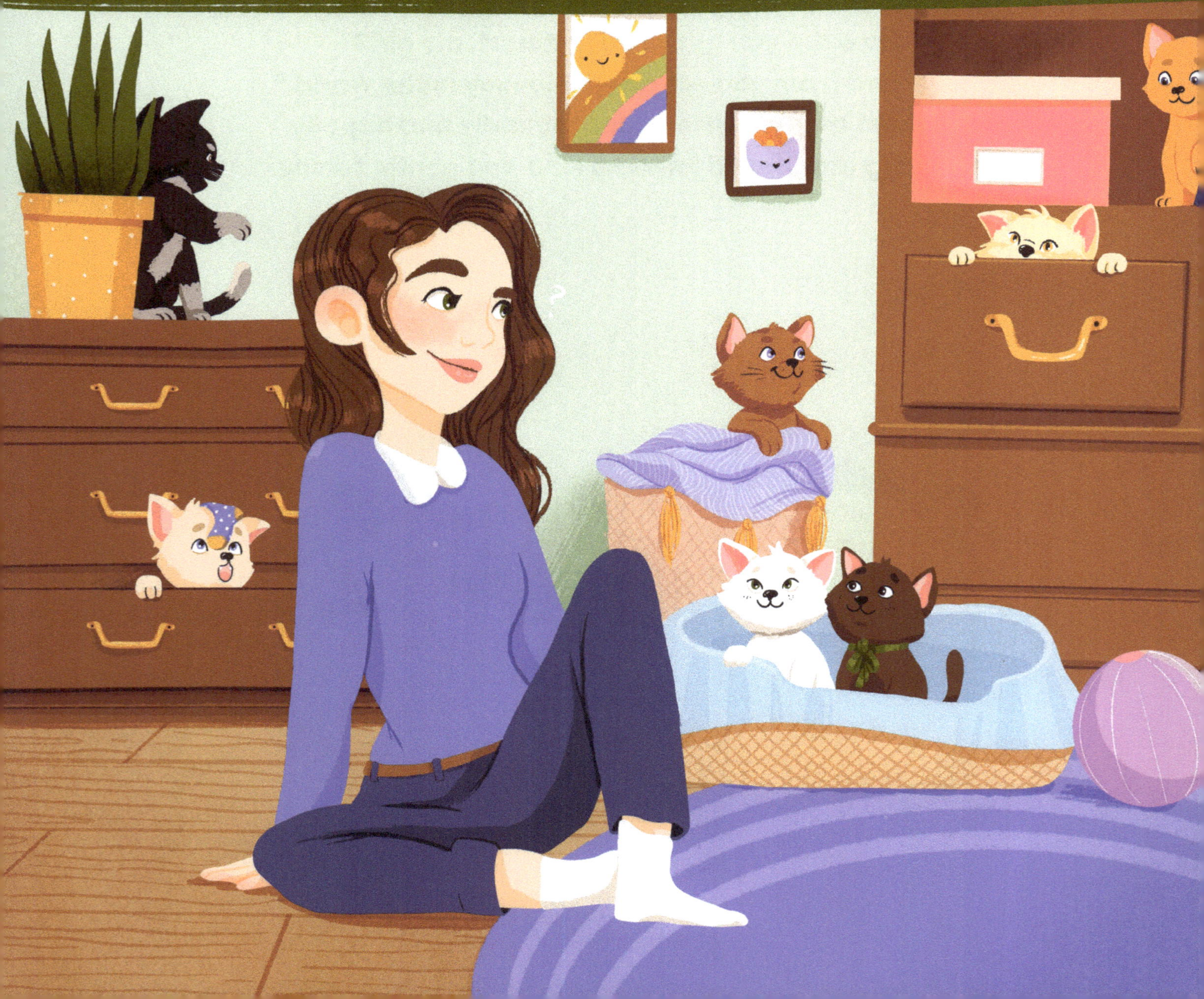

SINGLE MOM'S BUSY DAY SURVIVAL KIT

Quick healthy snack recipes,
5-minutes stress-relief tips,
and fun, easy activities to keep
your kids entertained so you
can catch your breath.

scan me for your free copy!

www.ingramcontent.com/pod-product-compliance
Lightning Source LLC
Chambersburg PA
CBHW051629140626
46547CB00033B/2960